GW01091227

Sammy's Magic Garden

A Ghost Musical

Kjartan Poskitt

Samuel French – London
New York – Sydney – Toronto – Hollywood

SAMMY'S MAGIC GARDEN

First presented at the Cathedral Hall, Edinburgh, in August 1985 sponsored by Yorkshire Television. It was produced by Clive Wolfe with the National Student Theatre Company, with the following cast of characters:

Sammy, a schoolboy	Paul Connelly
Alice, his best friend	Lon David
Egbert, Sammy's dad	Toby Scott
Gloria, Sammy's mum	Caroline Owens
Miss Nettle, the housekeeper	Maureen Glackin
Compost, the gardener	Ivan Kaye
Schoolfriends/Flower-children	Sally Beauchannon, Joanne Boddison, Dympna Clerkin, Melanie Jones, Meg McDonald

Directed and Designed by **Claudia Lloyd**
Musical Director **Simon Ellingham**

Sammy's Magic Garden was revised for its first professional production at The Polka Theatre, Wimbledon, on 21st June, 1989, with the following cast of characters:

Sammy, a schoolgirl	Josephine Melville
Eddie, her best friend	Ian Doody
Egbert	Joe Cushley
Gloria	Erika Poole
Miss Nettle	Lizzie Queen
Compost	Tony Pritchard
Schoolfriends/Flower-children	Daniella Borini, Rachael Ferguson, Laura Hayes, Frances Merivale, Louissa Nicola, Jonathan Norman, Patrick Saich, Desiree Senior

Directed by **Chris Fisher**
Designed by **Alex Bunn**
Musical Director **Nick Skilbeck**

CHARACTERS

Sammy Matthews, a schoolboy
Alice, Sammy's best friend
Egbert, Sammy's dad
Gloria, Sammy's mum
Miss Nettle, the housekeeper
Compost, the gardener
Sandra
Martin
Kevin
Bridget

Some of Sammy's schoolfriends

A chorus of schoolfriends/enchanted flower-children

SYNOPSIS OF SCENES

ACT I

ACT II

MUSICAL NUMBERS

ACT I

1	**Magic Garden Theme**	
2	**School Is Over**	Sammy and schoolkids
3	**Don't You Know What Happens To ...**	Miss Nettle
4	**The Weirdest Thing I've Ever Seen**	Compost
3a	**Don't You Know What Happens To ...** (reprise)	Miss Nettle
5	**Remember There's Nothing To Be Scared Of**	Compost
6	**Don't Go Into The Garden**	Compost

ACT II

7	**Catch The Cat**	Egbert, Gloria, and kids
8	**Flame Of Youth**	Egbert and Gloria
5a	**Remember There's Nothing To Be Scared Of** (reprise)	Sammy
9	**It's Nice To See You Again**	Flower-kids
10	**I'm Not Scared**	Sammy and Alice
	Finale Medley: Remember There's Nothing To Be Scared Of/I'm Not Scared	Company

The piano/vocal score is available on sale from Samuel French Ltd

PRODUCTION NOTE

As will be noted from the cast lists, the part of "Sammy" may be played as male or female. "Alice" may also become "Eddie" if required!

This particular text features four distinct speaking parts for Sammy's schoolfriends. However, the number of kids may be varied according to individual production requirements or restrictions.

Sadly, but for obvious reasons, it has not been practical to include any neat topical lines or references in this text. However, if one or two such additions should occur whilst mounting the production, I should be most disappointed if they were *not* slipped in!

Kjartan Poskitt

ACT I

SCENE 1

The Magic Garden Theme, Music 1, is played, the stage is dark. After the theme, a school handbell rings and all the schoolkids including Sammy and Alice bound on stage as it lights up to reveal the exterior of Sammy's house. It is a quaint yet slightly mysterious, large-looking building. They all sing the first number

Music 2: School Is Over

All
School is over for the day
Boy I'm glad to get away
And leave the teachers on their own
Now the lessons are all done
It's high time we had some fun
Tell my momma I'm a-coming home
English, Maths and History
fill my heart with sorrow
French is just a mystery
but who cares till tomorrow
No more gym or long division
No more science test revision
Tell my momma I'm a-coming home.

The music continues as Sammy talks over

Sammy (*to the audience*) Hello, I'm Sammy! I've just moved in here and these are all my schoolfriends I've met today. This is Alice who I sit next to.

Alice Hiya! So how'd you find school today, Sammy?

Sammy I just walked down the road and there it was behind the railings!

Alice Hey, screams of laughter!

The last lines of the song are repeated

All
English, Maths and History
fill my heart with sorrow
French is just a mystery
but who cares until tomorrow
No more gym or long division
No more science test revision
Tell my momma I'm a-coming home.

Sammy So now school's over, what do you lot get up to?

Sandra Lots of exciting things.

Sammy Like what?

Sandra Er, well, exciting things like, er . . . well go on, Martin, *you* tell him.
Martin Eh? Oh yeah! Um, I dunno, you decide.
Sandra Me? It's always me!
Sammy But there are lots of things to do round here, aren't there?
Sandra Masses.
Martin Yeah, tons.
Kevin I'm starving.
All but Kevin Shut up, Kevin!
Sammy So what will you be doing tonight?
Sandra Whatever it is, it's bound to be exciting.
Kevin Yeah! Like eating.
All but Kevin Shut up, Kevin!
Sandra You'll wear your jaw out one day.
Martin That'll be exciting.
Sandra Martin, tell Sammy what we're going to do.
Martin Kevin, you tell him.
Kevin Don't ask me! Ask Bridget.
All but Bridget Bridget, what are we going to do?
Bridget Homework.
Sammy How exciting!
Bridget Yes, teacher's given us some jolly interesting sums to do, and
there's a super essay on French verbs . . .

Other kids groan and wander off saying goodbye to Sammy

Alice and Bridget stay behind with Sammy

I think it's jolly exciting, Sammy. Isn't it, Alice?
Alice Rather, I certainly can't wait to start mine.
Bridget Me too. Well, I'll be off. See you.
Sammy }
Alice } *(together)* 'Bye!

Bridget exits

Alice So what's your new house like then, Sammy?
Sammy I haven't really had a chance to explore it yet. It's very big and old.
Do you want a look round? You can see all our packing cases!
Alice I can't really. I promised Mum I'd take Rover for a walk.
Sammy That won't take long.
Alice It will. Rover's a tortoise. I could come round later.
Sammy Really? Great, see you then.
Alice Hang loose, honey.

*Alice merrily bounds off, nearly knocking over Sammy's Dad, whose nose is
buried in a book, as usual*

Sammy Yet soft! Who approaches? Why 'tis none other than my noble dad.
Egbert Hmmm? Oh, hello Sammy. Who was that?
Sammy That was my new friend from school, Alice.
Egbert Spiffing.
Sammy Did you have a good day at work, Dad?

Egbert Brill, triff and fab. I think I've synthesised the molecular distortion of activated enzymes to a regrouping stage. I just need the catalytic ray converter now.

Sammy There now follow sub-titles in English ...

Egbert Eh?

Sammy (*to the audience*) Dad's an inventor you see, mega brainy aren't you, Dad?

Egbert Er, um. ...

Sammy For instance, what was the loudest pop concert in the world?

Egbert *Easy!* "The Who" at Charlton Athletic Stadium in nineteen seventy-six.

Sammy How many sandwiches can Princess Anne eat for dinner?

Egbert *Peasy!* Seven with a glass of orange.

Sammy Why are elephants big and grey?

Egbert *Easy peasy!* If they were small and yellow, they'd be lemons.

Sammy See? He knows everything!

Egbert Er, Sammy?

Sammy Yes, that's me, Dad.

Egbert I've forgotten which our new house is.

Sammy This one!

Gloria (*from inside*) Is that you, Egbert?

Egbert I think so.

Gloria (*off*) What do you mean, you think so?

Egbert I'm just checking in a mirror. Yes, it's me.

Gloria (*off*) Very funny. You come in here, and be sure to wipe your feet on the mat.

Egbert Is my tea on the table?

Gloria (*off*) No, it's in the teapot.

Sammy (*to the audience*) Does your family go on like this?

Egbert has slipped off his shoes and socks and is rubbing the door mat on his feet

Gloria appears

Gloria Egbert, what *are* you doing?

Egbert Wiping my feet on the mat, dear. Now then, tea.

Egbert potters inside, carrying his shoes and socks

Gloria Sammy, what are we going to do with him?

Sammy He's all right! (*To the audience*) This is my mum, everybody.

Gloria Hello!

Sammy Pretty, funny, intelligent, kind—just some of the things she calls me.

Gloria You! If cheek grew on trees, you'd be wooden.

Sammy Mother, you slay me.

Gloria Don't be long coming in, and wipe your feet too or Miss Nettle *will* slay you.

Sammy Who's Miss Nettle?

Gloria She's the housekeeper, and she's **very** fussy, so you mind your manners with her.

Sammy Don't I always?

Gloria No.

Gloria goes in

Sammy Oh! Well, you've met the family, **seen** the house and my new friends—you know as much as I do, now. I must say, everybody seems really nice. I think I'm going to like it here.

But ... Miss Nettle suddenly appears at the door. She rather ominously is sweeping the step with a broom

Nettle Who are you? Get away. Shoo, go on, off this door step.

Sammy But ...

Nettle But? *But?* You say *but* to me? I shall have none of your impertinence, child, be off with you.

Sammy But I live here.

Nettle "But I live here"! *Nonsense.*

Sammy I'm Sammy, we moved in yesterday.

Nettle *We?* Do you mean to say that a child is to live *here*?

Sammy In a manner of speaking ... but not really a child, more a sort of ... me!

Nettle A child!

Sammy You're Miss Nettle, I presume.

Nettle A presumptious child!

Sammy But I only meant ...

Nettle But, But, But! I hope very much you don't touch things that don't belong to you, child. And, you don't ever look in cupboards not meant for little boys, am I clear? In fact you just don't do anything at all ...

Sammy Mind if I breathe?

Nettle Yes.

Sammy Well, lovely to have met you.

Sammy sneaks past her into the house

Miss Nettle mutters to herself and the audience

Nettle Yeauchh! For years I've kept this house in order, it's been a tidy, clean, decent, respectable house for people to live in, and now *this*! Yet again a horrible noisy, squeaky little brat moves in, messing up here, touching this, moving that ... and the noise! Children just speak and behave as they wish these days. We were properly taught to respect our elders. Did you ever hear that children should be seen and not heard? Namby-pamby attitude! Children should be not seen *and* not heard, eh? *Eh?*

During her speech the opening music riff for her song has started. She now bursts into:

Music 3: Don't You Know What Happens To ...

(*Singing*)   Don't you know what happens to
Naughty children just like you?
They disappear and are never seen again
Those that shout and laugh and shriek
Those that tease and offer cheek
Those who lie and mumble and complain
Frosty winds of chilling white
will drag you from your bed at night
and hold you fast before a rising moon
There you'll stay until the dawn
when you'll find yourself reborn
All your friends will pass you by
but they won't hear you when you cry
So now you know what happens to
Naughty children just like you
They disappear and are never seen again.

The music continues as she talks over

(*Speaking*) And as for "But, but, but" Sammy Smartipants, I don't think he's going to last long at all. None of the others did. Get my drift?

She sings the last bit of the song again

(*Singing*)   Frosty winds of chilling white
will drag you from your bed at night
and hold you fast before a rising moon
There you'll stay until the dawn
when you'll find yourself reborn
All your friends will pass you by
but they won't hear you when you cry
So now you know what happens to
Naughty children just like you
They disappear and are never seen again.

Miss Nettle cackles and exits

Fade lights

SCENE 2

The lane behind the garden

Lights up as Compost the gardener enters

Compost Oooh, Arr! Hello y'all! Here, what's all these long faces? You look like you've just seen caterpillars on your prize marrows. Bet I know what's bothering you, it's that horrible Miss Nettle, isn't it? That woman can turn milk sour just by looking at it. My name's Compost by the way. I'm the gardener. Well, be friendly, say hello Compost then. . . . What's your names? . . . (*He encourages audience response*) Well my little bunch of blossoms, I ain't gonna remember all those, but you do look nice sitting there in your little rows, like a set of cabbage-patch dolls waiting for harvest. Anyway, I'd best be getting to work. The new people have just moved in and there's a lot to do. I was going to sow some potatoes today, but I can't. You're all meant to say "Why not, Compost?" . . . I'll try that again. I was meant to sow some potatoes today but I can't . . .

Audience response

. . . because I lost my needle and thread. Hur, hur, hur, that's my favourite joke at the moment, you'll be hearing it again later I expect. Right, time for me to be off to my potting shed. Do you know why I call it a potting shed? Because I made it out of a snooker table. Hur, hur, hur, that's my second favourite joke. Hello, who's this?

Sammy enters

Sammy Hello.
Compost Hello there.
Sammy Who are you?
Compost Compost. I'm the gardener.
Sammy I'm Sammy, I've just moved into the old house.
Compost Have you?
Sammy Yes. Something wrong?
Compost No, no, nothing. Er, did you meet Miss Nettle by the way?
Sammy Yes.
Compost What did you think of her?
Sammy I'm afraid she wasn't very nice.
Compost She's not very keen on young people. 'Ticularly ones that live in the old house. Didn't scare you at all, did she?
Sammy Oh no! (*To the audience*) Were we scared? (*Leading the response*) . . . No!
Compost So if it gets a bit scarier you don't mind?
Sammy Do we mind? (*Leading the response*) . . . No!
Compost Just as long as we have warned the mums and dads!
Sammy How do we get into the garden anyway? The back door's bricked up, and there's thick ivy all over the windows.
Compost Oh, you don't want to go in really.
Sammy I do. I like gardens.
Compost Not this one. There's nothing to look at.
Sammy You're just saying that because you've let it get overgrown, haven't you?
Compost No, I've just had a lot of trouble. I was going to sow some daffodil seeds today but I couldn't.
Sammy Why not?
Compost Because I couldn't find a needle and thread. Hur, hur.
Sammy Oh wow, mega funny. Come on, show me the way in.
Compost Look, it's better if I don't.
Sammy Why?
Compost You're going to think I'm being foolish, but the garden isn't a good place for young 'uns.

Sammy Gardens are great places for young 'uns!

Compost This one isn't! Please, for your own good . . .

Sammy I'm going in, so be a pal and show me the way . . . what is it that's bothering you?

Compost Put it like this.

Music 4: The Weirdest Thing I've Ever Seen

(*Singing*) In my life I've moved around
from place to place and town to town
I've been to China and to Mexico
I spent a day in Kathmandu
I've even been to Scunthorpe too
If a place is there I'm keen to go.
To me the globe is just a ball
and I can say I've done it all
I can't think of nowhere I ain't been
but though I've travelled far and wide
I tell you that that garden is the
weirdest thing that I have ever seen.
I can hardly show surprise
when right there before my eyes
a skeleton comes knocking on my door.
I've seen bananas coloured pink
occasionally I even think
there's something good to watch on Channel 4.
I have seen how Eskimos
say how are you with their nose
I've even seen a blackbird that was green
but all that's hardly worth a mention
when I tell you that that garden is the
weirdest thing I've ever seen.
I hope you won't complain
when I decline to explain
please don't be annoyed
when I tell you that that garden
is one thing you must avoid 'cause
On the Himalayan slopes
I saw magicians climbing ropes
and disappearing right into thin air.
I have seen the Japanese
try to microprocess cheese
I've even seen a snooker ball with hair.
So even though I've seen the lot
don't ask me how or why or what
please try to understand just what I mean
when I tell you keep away
because I warn you that that garden
is the weirdest thing I've ever
is the weirdest thing I've ever
is the weirdest thing I've ever seen.

Sammy But what's so weird about it?

Compost Look, perhaps one day I'll take you in and try to explain, but maybe not now, eh? I've got a few things to do in my potting shed.

Sammy Why's it called a potting shed?

Compost I was hoping you'd ask. Because I made it out of a snooker table. Hur, hur, hur.

Sammy Oh no!

Compost Oh yes! 'Bye for now.

Sammy 'Bye!

Compost toddles off

Sammy Well, there's an odd thing, I hope he shows me round soon, I want to see what's so weird. Anyway, I'd better get back, I've got lots of lovely homework to do. Yuck!

Fade lights

SCENE 3

In the living room, Egbert is sitting on the sofa reading a book, Gloria is next to him trying to watch the telly

Gloria It's no good, this telly still isn't working right. Come on Egbert, it's been a week now, can't you fix it?

Egbert It could be the aerial orientation.

Gloria Well, see to it, dear.

Egbert Yes, dear.

Still with his nose in his book, Egbert wanders round the room holding the telly aerial. Gloria is glued to the picture and doesn't watch him at all

Egbert Any better, dear?

Gloria No . . . oh, there was something. Do that again.

Egbert Where?

Gloria There, no keep it like that . . . a bit more, yes that's better . . . no, lost it, put it where it was, *no*—in between those . . . ah, that way! More . . . yes . . . good . . . keep it there . . . perfect . . . don't move it now.

Egbert has by now climbed onto the sideboard or table and is holding the aerial aloft, still reading his book

Sammy comes in

Sammy Hello Mum, what are you watching?

Gloria Oh, nothing special. I'll turn it off.

Sammy Why's Dad pretending to be the Statue of Liberty?

Gloria (*to Egbert*) What on earth are you doing up there?

Egbert Reading, dear.

Gloria Egbert Matthews! Get on down.

Sammy Hey man, let's *all* get on down, it's boogie time. C'mon daddy-oh, let's swing it!

Sammy and Egbert boogie

Egbert Hmmm, very groovy. Won't you join us, dear?
Gloria Honestly! (*To Sammy*) Haven't you got some homework to do?
Sammy Yes, and Alice is coming round, too.
Egbert What's the homework tonight then?
Sammy Quadrilateral equations.
Egbert Oh, goody. Let's see.
Sammy (*grabbing his books*) Mine, all mine, all mine.
Egbert Meany.
Gloria (*to Egbert*) You can come and help me in the kitchen.
Sammy Go on, if you're good I'll let you check them later.

There is a knock on the door

Sammy That'll be Alice.

Gloria goes to the door to let Alice in

  Alice enters

Gloria In you come, dear.
Alice Hi, everybody.
Egbert Sammy won't let me do his equations, Alice.
Alice Here's mine, help yourself!
Sammy No, Alice, he's got to learn it's a cruel, hard world and before he
  gets any equations, he's got to earn them in the kitchen.
Gloria Come on Egbert, you can help me with tea.
Egbert I bet Einstein never had to help with the tea.

  Off go the parents, leaving Sammy and Alice

Alice The house is looking a bit more together now, Sammy.
Sammy Alice, I've got to tell you something.
Alice What?
Sammy You're my best friend right? You'll listen?
Alice Brain to ears: Urgent announcement. Listen to Sammy. What's up?
Sammy Alice, there's something really weird about this place.
Alice Apart from your dad?
Sammy Alice, honest! To start with, there's a garden round the back that
  you can't get into. The gardener's really funny about it, saying it's
  dangerous, and so on.
Alice He just doesn't want you trampling over his prize begonias, I expect.
Sammy Then there's the housekeeper, Miss Nettle.
Alice I know her. She gives me the creeps.
Sammy She was going on about how awful it is having a child living here.
Alice You're not a child, Sam.
Sammy Well, thanks Alice! Anyway, odd little things keep happening.
Alice Like what?
Sammy Daft things. The lights come on at night, the stairs creak when
  there's nobody about, things keep falling off shelves.
Alice It'll be rats or something.

Sammy All right, how about this . . . this morning when I came downstairs
somebody had taken Dad's ancient old train set out of the box and fixed it
up on the floor, here.

Alice What did your mum say?

Sammy She thought I'd done it, but it wasn't me.

Alice Got it!

Sammy What?

Alice It must be the phantom train set player who comes out at midnight
and vents his cruel rage on innocent little trains . . .

Sammy All right, laugh, but it's a bit hard to explain.

Alice It'll be harder to explain if we haven't got this homework done by
tomorrow. Come on, we'll talk about this later.

Sammy You do believe me, don't you, Alice?

Alice Come on, let's do this. $2X(a+b)=4$ . . . $2X(a-b)=2$.

Egbert enters

Egbert Potty. Subtract the common factors, $4bX=2$ so $X=1$ over $2b$.

Sammy Oh, Dad!

*Gloria has come in and parked herself on the sofa. She slips off her slippers
and prepares for a nap*

Gloria Egbert, sit here and read quietly.

Alice That's one done. Fab.

Gloria Sorry, we won't disturb you again.

Alice That sort of disturbance is fine by me.

Gloria And Egbert . . .

Egbert Yes dear?

Gloria Be quiet. I'm sleepy with all this country air.

Egbert Yes, the higher ozone content affects the somnolent recesses of the
rear brain lobes inducing a state of drowsiness . . .

Gloria Quiet, Egbert.

Egbert Oh yes. Sorry. (*Turning to Sammy and Alice*) *Sorry!*

Sammy That's all right, Dad.

Egbert I'll read my book now.

Sammy You do that.

Egbert Jolly interesting.

Sammy Yes, Dad.

Egbert About the lost Mandoolie tribe, discovered in the Congo. Everybody thought that . . .

*Egbert is silenced by Gloria stuffing one of her slippers in his mouth. Gloria
dozes off, Egbert settles down with his book, Sammy and Alice chew their biros
thoughtfully, when suddenly*

Black-out. An eerie wind whispers in the background

Sammy Oh no, it's the lights again!

*Lights flicker back on. A large rag doll has appeared on the table at which
Sammy and Alice are working*

Sammy That's better.
Alice Oh, wow.
Sammy What?
Alice That doll wasn't there before!
Sammy It's a rag doll.
Alice Is it yours?
Sammy No. Yours?
Alice Hey, don't touch it! Maybe your dad threw it over.
Sammy Dad?
Egbert Hmm? (*Seeing the doll*) Golly, a dolly! Oh I haven't seen one of those in years. Your mother had one as a girl, Daisy she called it.
Gloria (*waking*) Egbert.
Egbert Sorry, dear.
Alice So how did it get there?
Sammy The phantom dolly-deliverer.
Alice Seriously, Sam!
Sammy See what I mean about odd things happening?
Alice Oh, real wow . . . ah!

Egbert looks up as the lights flicker again

Egbert That's probably the switching station changing supplies. Always causes a few surges.
Alice Oh.
Sammy Doesn't explain the doll though.
Alice A doll's not exactly scarey though, is it? If you've got a ghost that plays with dolls, it might be quite friendly anyway. It'd be pretty good to have a friend who was a ghost, don't you think?
Sammy Suppose so . . .

They try and settle down again, but the creepy wind noise is unnerving them. Then a nasty greenish hand comes through the curtains immediately behind the sofa where the parents are sitting

Alice *Sam!*

Sammy screams sharply and the hand goes away

Gloria Whatever's that?
Egbert Sounded like a scream, dear.
Gloria Sammy, are you all right?
Sammy Mum, behind the curtains . . .
Alice It was just there . . .
Gloria (*looking in vain*) What, where?
Sammy There was a hand, Mum, coming for you.
Egbert That's handy.
Gloria Yes, we all need a hand sometimes.
Sammy We both saw it, didn't we, Alice?
Gloria There, there, I think you are working too hard on these equations. Childish imagination, that's all.
Sammy Mum, we both saw it.

Alice We did!
Sammy (*to the audience*) Didn't we see it?

Audience response

See, I'm not childish.

Gloria Sammy Matthews, who but a child would get up in the middle of the night to play trains? Alice, I thought you'd be more sensible. Oh, look Egbert, Alice's brought a doll with her. I had one just like this you know.
Alice That's not actually mine, Mrs Matthews.
Gloria (*a bit concerned*) Sammy?
Sammy Come off it, Mum! It just appeared!
Gloria Rubbish, it's all in the mind.
Alice I can smell burning.
Gloria Hands, dolls, burning. Egbert, I'm afraid these children have been overworking.
Sammy I can smell it too.
Egbert (*taking his nose from his book*) Can you smell burning?
Gloria Don't you start, there's no . . . the oven! I forgot!

Gloria zooms out

Egbert Ha, ha. Go on, let's have a quick look at these sums.
Gloria (*off*) Egbert, get in here!
Egbert Oh, draggy scene, man.

Egbert goes off muttering

Sammy Well?
Alice We didn't imagine it?
Sammy They saw it too. (*To audience*) Didn't you?
Alice Were you scared?

Audience response

Sammy I don't know if we'll get this homework done now.

A clock chimes nine

Alice That clock's a bit fast.
Sammy There's something really wrong there.
Alice Oh come on, clocks are often fast.
Sammy No, Alice. We haven't got a clock.

They pause for a second to digest the implications of this

Miss Nettle comes on and notices them

Nettle Not in bed yet?
Sammy This is all we need.
Nettle (*sniffing*) And *what* have you brats been up to now?
Sammy The kitchen caught fire.
Nettle There's a place for filthy little beasts like you, and it's not here.
Sammy Where are you going, anyway?

Nettle I've been with this house a great deal longer than you and I shall come and go as I please without your impertinent questions, thank you. What's the matter with that little girl?

Sammy We just saw something a bit strange, that's all.

Nettle Oh, really? Well maybe you think I'm old fashioned, but children setting fire to kitchens is a bit strange to me!

Sammy
Alice } (*together*) We didn't!

Nettle It never caught fire before you came here.

Sammy But, but ...

Nettle But, but, but again! ... This house doesn't like children, and it certainly has no need of those who tell lies!

Sammy We aren't lying! It was just ...

But Miss Nettle has seen and picked up the mysterious rag doll on the table

Nettle What are you doing with this?

Alice Nothing.

Nettle Where did you get it?

Alice It just appeared.

Sammy The lights flickered and ...

Nettle Did I tell you to keep away from the scullery cupboard?

Sammy It's locked anyway.

Nettle So you *have* tried it?

Sammy No, you said ...

Nettle A thief and a liar!

Music 3a: Don't You Know What Happens To ... (Reprise)

(*Singing*)   Don't you know what happens to
Thieves and liars just like you?
There's a special place for them to go
There they rot their lives away
Freeze by night and burn by day
No one cares and no one wants to know.

The music continues as Miss Nettle shakes the doll in front of Sammy. The doll has a little bell in it which tinkles. Sammy is hypnotised by the doll. Miss Nettle mockingly addresses Alice

If I were you, little girl, I'd keep well away from little Mr Sammy Smartipants here; something nasty is liable to happen to him.

She twists the rag doll about violently and Sammy's body copies the movements of the doll. He slumps to the ground groaning. Alice gets down to see if he's all right

Miss Nettle cackles and exits with the doll

Enormous echoing footsteps are heard approaching, Alice helps Sammy to hide. They cower under the table together

The footsteps stop as Compost comes on

Compost (*to the audience*) Hello, my little Jersey Royals. Say "Hello, Compost!"

Audience reaction

Thank you. Now then, have you seen young Sammy?

Audience reaction

Where? Oh, and Alice too? What are you two doing under there?

Sammy Alice was scared.

Alice I thought you were.

Compost I think you both were. What's up?

Sammy It's her.

Compost It certainly looks like her.

Sammy No, Miss Nettle. She's a witch or something.

Compost A witch?

Alice Yeah, wow she's weird. She says really awful things.

Compost But I say awful things too.

Sammy ⎫
            ⎬ (*together*) You do?
Alice ⎭

Compost Believe it, if I'm banging in a nail with a hammer and I hit my thumb, I say some terrible things.

Sammy No, she was threatening us, and there were these hands that appeared, and a doll.

Alice And when she twisted the doll up, Sammy went all funny.

Compost Now then, you know what happens to people who tell lies, don't you?

Sammy Don't you start.

Alice Honest, she just twisted this doll . . .

Sammy It was a rag doll, with yellow hair and a red dress . . .

Compost (*suddenly serious*) Oh.

Sammy You know it?

Compost It's Lucinda's doll.

Alice Who's Lucinda?

Compost She used to live here.

Sammy Did she move?

Compost In a manner of speaking, yes she moved.

Sammy What can we do about Miss Nettle, then?

Compost Look, did she do anything but frighten you?

Alice She was making Sammy go freaky.

Compost Just frightened you though, eh?

Sammy ⎫
            ⎬ (*together*) Yes.
Alice ⎭

Compost Don't you worry then, being frightened's just a piece of nonsense. It only happens when you don't understand what's going on.

Music 5: Remember There's Nothing To Be Scared Of

(*Singing*)   If you hear a creaking in the night
it's only a skeleton touching his toes
if a cold breeze then gives you a fright
it's only a werewolf blowing his nose
if you hear a tapping on the window
if you hear a rapping on the door
it could be a spook or a vampire bat
but it won't be anything worse than that.
If you find a phantom in your kitchen
he probably just wants something to eat
If you feel your nose is itching
it's an invisible monster with smelly feet
and if you're climbing up the staircase
and a ghost comes into view
take a deep breath, shout out "Boo!"
he'll be a lot more frightened than you.
Remember there's nothing to be scared of
Remember there's nothing there at all
Remember there's nothing to be scared of
Remember there's nothing there at all

Gloria enters

Gloria Hello, Compost.
Compost Evening, Mrs Matthews.
Gloria Tea's ready for you two, if you'd like to come through.
Compost There, your old mum'll look after you.
Gloria *Old?* Gee, thanks.
Sammy She worships us, you know.
Compost How do you know?
Sammy She's about to put a burnt offering in front of us.

Gloria, Sammy and Alice exit

Compost Ahhh! Here, I'll have to admit I'm a bit concerned. Funny things happen to children that live here, and I'm sure that Miss Nettle has something to do with it. She don't scare me mind, but it can be upsetting for the kiddies.

On comes the much-maligned Miss Nettle

Nettle You, gardener, what are you doing here? Shouldn't you be in your potting shed?
Compost I bet you don't know why it's called a potting shed?
Nettle Why?
Compost Because I made it out of a snooker table! Hur, hur, hur, hur, hur.

Fade lights

SCENE 4

Lights up. It is the next day. Outside school, Sammy meets Alice

Sammy Hello Alice, did you get your homework done?
Alice Just about. How much did you write for the geog essay?
Sammy A page and a half.
Alice Two pages. No bother.
Sammy Well *nyah* to you. Oh look, here comes the cavalry.

Sandra, Martin and Kevin come on

Sammy }
Alice } (*together*) Hello Sandra, Martin and Kevin.
Sandra }
Martin } (*together*) Hello Sammy and Alice.
Kevin }
Sammy How much did you write for your geog essay?
Sandra Just under a page. That was with big writing too.
Martin Just under just under a page.
Sandra What about you, Kevin?
Kevin Geog essay? Ooooops.
Martin Haven't you done one?
Sandra He can always say he ate it.

Bridget come on with a massive amount of paper

All (*seeing Bridget*) Oh no!
Sandra Is that all your essay?
Bridget No!
All Phew!
Bridget I couldn't carry the rest.
Martin What did you find to write about?
Bridget There's masses of stuff. Haven't you brought yours?
Sammy Here's mine.
Bridget Let's see. Hmm, this is odd. (*Reading*) "For pity's sake, please help us, we are trapped ..."
Sammy What's that?
Bridget Your essay. The bit in red.
Sammy Red?
Alice Look, "For pity's sake, please help us, we are trapped by the phantom of the magic sundial." What's that about, Sam?
Sammy Oh, it's a sort of joke I put in for the teacher.
All but Sammy Eh?

The school bell goes

Bridget Hooray! School time. Come on, we'll be late!
Sandra Last one in's a stinky poo.

The other kids run off moaning, leaving Sammy. He calls Alice back

Sammy Alice!

Alice OK, I'm interested. What's with the weird joke?

Sammy I never wrote this! Look, it's not my writing. (*Pointing*) This is, but this isn't. It's all dark red and blotchy.

Alice Was it there yesterday?

Sammy No, it must have got written in last night.

Alice I bet it's that Miss Nettle woman.

Sammy Er . . . maybe, I suppose.

Alice Come on, we'd better go. Sam? *Come on!*

Fade lights

SCENE 5

The Magic Garden Theme (Music 1) is played as the lights come up to reveal the kitchen. There is a large central table covered by a cloth with lots of bowls of gunge on in them, as well as scales, ladles, etc. Gloria is in her apron. Egbert is immersed in the cookery book

Gloria Egbert, will you please come here and concentrate?

Egbert Hmm? Oh yes. Why are we having all these cakes anyway?

Gloria It's the party, dear. Our son's birthday, remember? We're inviting all Sammy's new friends to celebrate and see the new house.

Egbert Can't they see it from the outside? Then we don't have to make cakes.

Gloria Egbert Matthews, will you take your nose out of that book and just help a little?

Egbert Right, dear.

Compost trundles himself on

Compost (*to the audience*) Hello, my little row of radishes.

Audience reaction

Gloria Compost, are you busy?

Compost Well, I was going to sow some turnip seeds today. (*To the audience*) Wait for it . . .

Gloria So why don't you?

Compost (*leading the audience*) I couldn't find a needle and thread. It gets funnier every time!

Gloria Well then, you can give us a hand! Come in.

Compost Well, I ain't really supposed to be in the kitchen . . .

Gloria Nonsense, find an apron.

Compost All right. So tell me, what is afoot?

Egbert It's a funny-shaped thing on the end of your leg.

Compost But aren't those cakes I smell?

Egbert They are and you do.

Gloria We're making cakes. It's Sammy's birthday next week.

Compost That sounds like fun.

Gloria Splendid, now where does Miss Nettle keep everything?

She opens a cupboard and a bag of flour or something falls on her. Compost laughs and she flicks some at him. He dives round the table and knocks Egbert who gets something on him. Gloria starts giggling and generally they start flicking bits of stuff about and chucking eggs and squirting icing mixture and having a good time. This gets more carried away until they have huge blots of mess on them

Sadly one extra huge blot hits Miss Nettle as she storms in

The three stand there very sheepishly

Gloria Oh, Miss Nettle! Your lovely dress! We *are* sorry!

Nettle What on earth do you think you're doing?

Gloria Well, actually we were making cakes, Miss Nettle.

Egbert and Compost are edging behind Gloria

Nettle (*to Egbert and Compost*) Where are you going?

Egbert Just coming to stand over here.

Nettle You stand right where you are. May I make something plain? In *my* kitchen I make the cakes.

Gloria Your kitchen? It is ours, Miss Nettle, it's our house. Tell her, Egbert.

Egbert Yes, er, you see, under the currently applicable terms of the nineteen thirty-two purchase act, the acquirer of the property shall be deemed the owner in so far as . . .

Nettle Who cleans? Who scrubs? Who polishes?

Gloria We'll clear this up, it won't take a minute . . .

Nettle Oh I see! You're going to do it so that's all right, is it? Do you know how many years I've spent keeping this kitchen tidy? Pointless years? Could I reasonably expect even the smallest amount of thanks? It seems not. Instead I come in here to find . . . this! No one ever treated *my* kitchen in this manner before. If a child had done this I'd have him beaten till he screamed. But you, the parents, the supposed example the child is to follow, I don't suppose you'd agree to that, would you? "Oh go and tip up the kitchen, cover Miss Nettle in mess why don't you? After all, she's only the servant . . ." . . . When I was a girl I spent hours standing facing the wall with a book on my head. It did me no harm and wouldn't have done you any harm either. And it would certainly have given you the sense of propriety you so obviously lack. (*To Compost*) As for you, gardener, you, in here! Trampling in your soil and other substances I've no doubt . . .

Gloria We invited him in to help, and anyway, I promise we'll have this clean in no time.

Nettle Will you? Will you really? I doubt it.

Gloria What do you mean?

Miss Nettle is fingering her odd brooch. We hear a spooky wind start up

Nettle Maybe you don't appreciate how hard it is to keep a kitchen clean, but you will. You will.

Miss Nettle storms out

Magic wind noises build up. The three look at each other, rather perplexed. It may be possible to arrange a few objects to mysteriously fly off shelves and so on as the lights go down

SCENE 6

Sammy's bedroom. Sammy is in bed writing in his diary

Sammy Tuesday ... eleventh after Epiphany, full moon, high tides at Margate eight-oh-three am and six-twelve pm. So what? (*To audience*) Oh, hello! I'm just doing my diary. So much seems to be happening these days. Before we moved here all I had in was like—Thursday, went to school; Friday, went to school. Saturday, didn't go to school. I haven't space for all the things that happen now. The train set, the garden, Miss Nettle and that doll, oh and Alice. There's too much. I'll just put "went to school".

Gloria comes on. She can be in a dressing gown

Gloria Are you in bed, Sammy?
Sammy Yes, Mum.
Gloria So what have you put in your diary today?
Sammy It's a secret.
Gloria I bet you put "went to school".
Sammy Huh! Mum, have you seen the garden here?
Gloria No, I've been far too busy.
Sammy I tried to but Compost wouldn't let me.
Gloria He was probably busy with something.
Sammy Not really, Mum, and anyway you must have noticed a lot of odd things happening.
Gloria No.
Sammy Come on, Dad's train set for one thing.
Gloria You must have sleep-walked.
Sammy Sleep-walked maybe, but sleep-putting up a train set is a bit unlikely. Anyway, you must find Miss Nettle a bit off.
Gloria Yes, well she's a very busy woman and has a lot to do, so don't you go upsetting her.
Sammy I don't, she just has it in for me and Alice. She even thought it was us that set fire to the kitchen the other night.
Gloria I'm sure that was just her joke.
Sammy Huh, even Compost's jokes are funnier than that.
Gloria You're all excited from being in a new place, it's just childish imagination again.
Sammy It's not.
Gloria I've seen nothing that proves anything. Now go to sleep and good night.
Sammy Mum, I've some proof, look!

Sammy reaches for his satchel which is hanging over the end of his bed

Gloria What is it? Don't say you got ten out of ten for your homework, that *is* weird.

Sammy I was going to school this morning and my essay had changed into a message. I couldn't show teacher, I had to pretend I'd forgotten to do it. Look.

Gloria flicks through the proffered book, then reads

Gloria "The extinction of the Dinosaur. Dinosaurs lived on earth for many millions of years, but suddenly they all died out. Nobody yet knows why . . ."

Sammy Let me see. That's just my essay! The message was just there, asking for help, honest, right there it was!

Gloria I'm sure, now go to sleep, Sammy.

Sammy I knew you wouldn't believe me.

Gloria What is there to believe? Come on, lights off and sleep.

Gloria goes

The lights go down and Sammy tries to sleep for about three seconds, then gives up

Sammy (*to the audience*) They never believe me. That letter in my homework was definitely there, wasn't it? I know it was. I wonder what time it is?

The clock chimes midnight

I'd love to know where that chiming's coming from. What do you think that message meant: "We are trapped by the phantom of the magic sundial."?

Distant thunder rumbles. Eerie wind noise starts

Thunder! Better try and sleep, I suppose.

Very distant voices are heard in the wind. They seem to be sighing "Help us". Sammy sits up again

Can you hear that? That's it, I'm going to see what's going on. I can hear somebody moving about. Maybe it's a burglar. I'd better take something.

Sammy removes a sheet from the bed and then stands in wait, holding the sheet above his head, resembling a typical ghost. The only light is on him

Compost creeps on

Compost turns and sees the "ghost". He emits a gasp. Sammy pounces and covers Compost with the sheet

Got you!

Compost Ow!

Sammy (*to the audience*) At least it's not a ghost, they don't go "Ow" when you biff them.

Lighting increases gradually till end of scene

Compost Go easy, that's enough.
Sammy Eh?
Compost I said "Go easy", Sammy!
Sammy Compost, what are you doing here?
Compost I can't tell you.
Sammy Of course you can, and what's all the odd noises?
Compost They're from the garden. Look, Sammy, please, get back to bed and forget you saw anything.
Sammy Forget this? You're joking. I'm coming with you.
Compost Sammy, please, something could happen to you.
Sammy Huh, I've come this far, I want to know what's up at least. Listen, those voices! Which way is it?

By now the eerie wind is overtaken by the spooky voices singing:

Voices   Help us and save us all . . .

This forms the background riff to the song which the desperate Compost breaks into:

Compost Sammy . . .

                    Music 6: Don't Go Into The Garden
   (Singing)   Don't go into the garden
                    Who knows what you are going to find there
                    Don't go into the garden—No
                    Something is quite peculiar
                    I say that you should try to avoid it
                    Don't go into the garden—No
Sammy *(speaking)* Why?
Compost *(singing)* I don't want to have to tell you
                    'bout the crazy things I've seen
                    Even if I could explain you'd think I was
                    mad
                    Curiosity will get you
                    better that you don't know at all
                    Don't go into the garden—Please.
Sammy *(insistently)* *Come on.*
Compost *(giving in)* This way then.

The lights fade and the music drops down into the backing voices again, as the scene becomes

                              SCENE 7

The Magic Garden (preferably achieved by backlighting a gauze and flying it). For a short while Sammy and Compost stand at the side of the stage, observing the unnaturally large flowers which are swaying to the music, which continues underneath

Sammy Look at those flowers.

Compost Don't touch them.
Sammy Why not?

Sammy has reached out and the nearest flower shies quickly away

Compost That's why.
Sammy What are they?
Compost All right, Sammy, listen. There's a curse on the house. Every child
 that's come to live under this roof falls under a spell and disappears.
Sammy Disappears?
Compost Not completely.
Sammy So where do they go then?
Compost Here!
Sammy But . . .
Compost Don't you see? These are the children. Some of them have been
 here for years, and there's only me to look after them. That's why I never
 let anyone in here.
Sammy Who did this? Who?

Compost refuses to say

 It's that Miss Nettle! Why won't you say it?

*Sammy goes over to stand next to the flowers and stares closely at them. They
murmur slightly. We see that in fact they are like mutant vegetation adopting
human form. At first, over the music, they only make a whispering, rustling
noise*

Sammy reaches out to try and touch one

Compost Watch out!
Sammy Why! Ahh!

*In turning to speak to Compost he brushes one. It lets out an odd cry which is
echoed around the others as if they are all part of one organism. They start to
move slightly*

Compost Under a full moon they can partially return to their normal state;
 that's why I'm here tonight. Sammy, be still!

*One by one the Flower-children start talking softly as if reproducing a voice
from the past. The others tend to echo the words continuously, building into a
weird barrage of hushed voices*

Flower-child 1 Be up the stair well lest your father come home.
Flower-child 2 The curtain is drawn, is the candle lit, ma?
Flower-child 3 The boys will be back before Michaelmas Night!
Flower-child 4 But for a penny the knife-grinder calls!
Sammy What are they saying?
Compost It's echoes from their past, but I wonder if they remember.
Sammy Look!

The Flower-children cease their odd words and start to move a little more

Compost They've sensed you're here.

Sammy Can they see me?
Compost They don't see or hear, in their darkness, they just know.

Sammy warily goes over to them, trying to be brave

Sammy (*feeling he has to shout*) Hello!

The Flower-children all shy away and moan grotesquely

Compost Shh! Let them read your mind!
Sammy (*whispering*) Hello! I know you can't hear me, but I'm here to help
you! Can you understand? I'm going to get you out of this! I'll do
something!
Compost What can you do?
Sammy There is a way! I'll find it! Have hope! Do you understand me, I'm
going to save you!

*The music and effects fade down and then the Flower-children start whispering
slowly, in staggered unison*

Flower-children You'll be next! You'll be next! Next! Next! *NEXT!*

The music builds up again and the lights go down to end Act I

INTERVAL

*During the Interval Alice goes round the audience and gets them to sign a giant
birthday card for Sammy. The card is then left somewhere convenient at the
side of the stage*

ACT II

SCENE 1

The Magic Garden Theme (1) is briefly played as Sammy enters. It's the living room and it's empty and dark. Sammy puts a table lamp on

Sammy Hello? Mum? *Mum?* Dad? I'm home. Mum. Dad. Cat, dog, goldfish? Hello dining room, I'm home. Yes, it is my birthday, thanks for remembering. Yes, I think I will celebrate by doing my homework. (*To the audience*) I hate it when there's nobody about. Oh, well.

Alice and all the school kids suddenly leap out of nowhere. The lights go up full. Music riff quietly starts

Kids SURPRISE!
Sammy Yaaaaah! What, eh?
Alice It's a surprise party.
Sammy Party? Why?
Alice For your birthday.
Sammy You remembered! Excellento. What shall we do first?

Kids all generally shout "dancing", "pass the parcel", "duck for apples", "cowboys and indians", "Trivial Pursuit", etc.

Bridget Homework.
All but Bridget What?
Bridget I said . . .
All but Bridget We know.
Alice It's *your* party, what do *you* fancy, Sammy?
Sammy Let's just cut a slice of rug and dance, Alice baby.
Sandra How about breakdancing?
All but Sandra Too dangerous.
Martin How about rock and roll?
All but Martin Too energetic.
Kevin How about soup and roll and butter?
All but Kevin Urrr! Kevin!

Egbert has crept on. Gloria follows

Egbert Ahem!
Sammy Dad!

Music 7: Catch The Cat

Egbert   I remember when I was a kid
                       The one big dance that we all did
                       Made everybody look and say what is that?

Is it twist or rock and roll,
Is it blues or is it soul?
We said we just call it "Catch the Cat".

Others (*speaking*)   What?

Egbert and Gloria then do the chorus with the hand action

Egbert
Gloria } (*together*)   You go
Here kitty here kitty here kitty kitty kitty
Here kitty here kitty kitty here here
Here kitty here kitty here kitty kitty kitty
Here kitty here kitty kitty here here

Gloria   One night at the high school dance
Teacher caught us holding hands
He said "Hey you two, enough of that".
We said "Sir it's not our faults,
we were never taught to waltz,
the only thing we know is 'Catch the Cat'".

Egbert
Gloria } (*together*)   You go
Here kitty here kitty . . . (*etc.*)

Gradually the kids start to pick up the hand movements, then Gloria and Egbert go into the fancy bit

Egbert (*speaking to the kids*) Keep it going.

Egbert
Gloria } (*together*)   All you need is a little syncopation
All it takes is a little concentration
All together in a tight formation
That's how to Catch the Cat
How to Catch the Cat.

All   Here kitty here kitty . . . (*etc.*)

Repeat from "All you need . . ." to the end with everyone singing and doing the fancy bit together then finish

Egbert What a good party. Now what shall we do?
Bridget Homework.
Egbert Oh, good.
All but Bridget and Egbert Oh, bad.
Gloria Come on, Egbert, we've got sandwiches and things to make.
Egbert I bet Elvis Presley never had to make sandwiches.

Gloria and Egbert go off

Sammy Now what, eh?
Sandra Aren't you going to show us around?

The kids generally agree this would be a neat idea

Sammy If you like. What do you want to see first?

Kids all generally shout out: upstairs, cellar, bedrooms, attic, lavatory, sauna, garden—ah yes, the garden

Sammy Oh, a bit dodgy is the garden.
All but Sammy Why?
Sammy There's some weird things in there.
All but Sammy Like what?
Sammy It's hard to explain.
Alice One time when I was here, we saw this horrible hand appear.
Sammy My dad's old train set starts going by itself at night.
Alice And there's this weird rag doll that appears out of nowhere.
Others Rubbish!
Alice Honest.
Sammy Like, remember that odd homework essay I had?
Bridget You mean the thing about a sundial?
Sammy I never wrote that.
Sandra So what's that got to do with the garden?
Sammy There's a sort of ghost that does these things, and *that's* where it
   lives.
Sandra Oh yeah? Woo, woo, I'm the ghost of a cabbage that got horribly
   eaten one hundred years ago today.
Martin I'm the ghost of a worm.
Kevin But now, the return of the phantom lettuce chomper!
All but Sammy, Alice, and Kevin Is it a bird?
Kevin No!
All but Sammy, Alice, and Kevin Is it a snail?
Kevin No, it's Dracularva, the undead caterpillar.
Alice Hey, come on you lot. It's Sammy's party after all.
Others Sorry, Sammy.
Sandra It is a bit hard to take seriously, though.
Sammy It's all right, it's just that ...

Black-out

There is a general shout of "What is it?"

Martin Probably just a power cut.
Kevin Whooo!

The lights come up and Bridget does a brief scream

Kevin That was just me fooling about, Bridget.
Sammy Are you O.K.?
Kevin Bridget, I'm sorry.
Alice Oh wow. Look who's turned up.

Alice has seen the doll which is sitting on the sofa

Sammy The doll!
Bridget Where did that come from?

*The kids start saying excitedly "But we were all over here". Sammy hushes
them*

Sammy Do you want to hear the whole story?

The others nod/agree eagerly

This place has a curse on it you see, it's haunted by all the kids who've lived here.

Everyone murmurs their concern

That's why the doll appears. It belongs to a girl called Lucinda who was here and it explains my train set going and so on.

Sandra What's it got to do with the garden?

Sammy It's where the kids are, they've all been turned into giant flowers.

Others Flowers?

Sammy I've seen them, they come alive.

Martin How, though?

Sammy Well, I maybe shouldn't tell you this but ... (*He stops as:*)

Miss Nettle comes on with a huge cake

Nettle Hello little children! Having a lovely party? I heard you making lots of noise and jumping about, so I've made you this cake. I do hope you'll all have a piece, especially you, Sammy. (*Her hideous grin suddenly falters as she sees the doll*)

Nettle Oh, the doll! Found it in my cupboard again, did you?

Sammy No!

Nettle Don't tell tales. Anyway, you *will* all have some cake, won't you?

Kevin Yes, please.

All but Kevin and Sammy Me too.

Sammy (*butting in*) Er ... Miss Nettle, we don't want to make a mess of crumbs on the carpet for you, so could you be a big pal and get a few plates?

Nettle Oh, all right. I'll be your BIG PAL, but don't any of you go away now.

She scoots off in a huff

Kevin grabs a slice of cake and is about to eat it

Kevin This is nice of her; I thought she hated us.

Sammy Don't!

Sammy snatches the cake

Kevin Eh, what's up?

Sammy Shhh! (*Whispering*) I was just trying to tell you, Miss Nettle is a witch!

Sandra (*blurting out*) Miss Nettle's a wi—

Sammy claps his hand over Sandra's mouth

Sammy Why else does she suddenly make a cake and be nice to us for the first time in ages? Because we're all together, and she can get us all at once.

All but Sammy and Alice You mean ...?

Alice Yes, it's her chance to pull off the end of childhood as we know it.

All but Sammy and Alice You mean ...?

Sammy The cake is poisoned!

Kevin recoils from the cake

Kevin Urghhhh!
Sammy I'm sorry, I maybe shouldn't have told you.
Sandra That's O.K.
Martin No, it's not. Actually, I've suddenly got to go home.
Kevin Me too.
Sandra And me, I've got a lot of homework to do.
Bridget Lucky thing, I've only got two essays and ten sums to do.
Sandra Wanna do mine?
Bridget If you really don't mind.
Sammy Are you really all going?

All sheepishly agree "Better do", "You know how it is", etc.

Alice I'll stay for a while.
Sammy Good. Come on, let's see the others out.

  The others all go off

  From the other way Egbert comes on with a bottle of pop

Egbert Here kitty, kitty, here kitty, kitty? Who wants some pop? Well, I
  suppose I do really. They must be playing hide-and-seek. All right, I'm
  coming. (*He starts swigging pop and looking under cushions and things*)
  Hello? Hmm, not there. Not *there*, either. (*He sees the cake*) My! What a
  smashing cake!
Gloria (*off*) Egbert, what are you doing?
Egbert Playing hide-and-seek with a bit of cake, dear. (*He has a slice and is
  holding it just by his mouth*) Now I see you . . . and now . . . (*He's just about
  to bite it when*)
Gloria (*off*) *Egbert!*
Egbert Yes, dear?
Gloria (*off*) Why have you put the sausage rolls in the freezer?
Egbert Because there wasn't any room in the oven.

Every time he's about to bite the cake, Gloria interrupts

Gloria (*off*) Of course there's room in the oven. And Egbert?
Egbert Yes?
Gloria (*off*) What did you do with the ice-cream?
Egbert I just stuck it somewhere out of the way.
Gloria (*off*) Congratulations, Egbert!
Egbert Thank you, dear. What for?
Gloria (*off*) It's the first time I've seen burnt ice-cream.
Egbert I'm so pleased for you.
Gloria (*off*) *Get in here!*

  *Egbert replaces the uneaten piece of cake and grumbles his way to the
  kitchen*

Compost enters

Compost (*to the audience*) Hello, my little snowdrops.

Audience reaction

Where's this party then? Not very groovy, is it? I've seen more life in a dung heap. Sammy? Alice? Where is everybody?

Sammy and Alice come back

Sammy They went home.
Alice That Miss Nettle ruined everything.
Compost Did she scare them all off?
Sammy Sort of.
Compost Didn't scare you though?
Sammy
Alice } (*together*) No.
Sammy (*to the audience*) Did she scare you?

Audience reaction

Alice (*to the audience*) We could do with a few more tough friends like you lot.
Compost Listen, I've something to tell you about her. You know my little friends in the garden? I think I know how she's doing it. I've caught her creeping into the garden late at night and acting very suspiciously. What do you say we wait up and catch her at it?
Sammy Yeah!
Alice Does that mean we could save the others?
Compost We can but try, you see . . .

Miss Nettle reappears

Nettle Here's the plates, Sammy! Where have all your dear little friends gone?
Sammy They had to go home, you see.
Nettle All of them?
Sammy They were sorry.
Nettle And what are you three whispering about so intently?
Alice Oh, nothing.
Sammy Nothing at all, just admiring the cake, really.
Nettle Have some then.
Sammy No! It, er, looks too good to eat. Anyway, my tummy's getting too fat.
Alice Yes, you'll have to diet.
Sammy Diet? What colour? Ha, ha, ha.

Miss Nettle is staring unpleasantly at this charade. Sammy and Alice are aware of this

Sammy Fancy a spot of jolly old homework, Al old pal?
Alice Spiffers, Sam, old man. Let's retire to the study.

Sammy I say, after you.
Alice Jolly dee, old fruit.

They scram

Compost is thinking hard

Compost Diet what colour? Oh, DYE IT! Hur, hur, I see now. You could dye it green, say. A green tummy, hur, hur. A green tummy might suit you, Miss Nettle, seeing as how you're called Miss Nettle.
Nettle You would do well to be careful.
Compost Oh, go and pickle your parsnips. Say, it is a nice cake that.
Nettle That's not for you, gardener.
Compost Well I may as well eat some if they've gone to paint their tummies.
Nettle You just leave that cake alone.
Compost That's just like you. Making a cake for Sammy's birthday then not letting anybody have any.
Nettle If you must know, it's my birthday too.
Compost You? Birthday? You were never born like normal people, were you?
Nettle You mind your manners, gardener!
Compost You don't scare me. We're going to fix you, so there.
Nettle What was it you were saying to those snivelling juveniles?
Compost Wouldn't you like to know? Safe to say they'll never trust you.
Nettle And why not?
Compost Because you're a mean, horrid, selfish, nasty, unpleasant, anti-social, bad-tempered, domineering, repugnant, greedy, uncooperative, twisted, evil old bat.
Nettle Is that all?
Compost And you won't let me have a piece of birthday cake.
Nettle There, there. All right, you can have a piece of cake if you like.
Compost Maybe I don't want a bit now.

Miss Nettle has slipped a bit on a plate and is starting to soft soap Compost into eating it

Nettle Go on. Here, it's good for you.
Compost No.
Nettle Come on, I know we've had our differences, but just this once, for my birthday ... A nice big piece of cake with an extra sweetie on top.
Compost I suppose it smells all right.
Nettle Go on, just give it a little taste!
Compost No, you're trying to get round me and it won't work.
Nettle All right then, please yourself. See if I care.

She slowly turns her back and Compost immediately takes a bite. She turns round quickly and he looks innocent

Nettle You'll miss the lovely chocolate filling.
Compost S'lemon.
Nettle There, you *did* try a bit. Not so bad, was it? Go on, have some more. Do you like that?

Compost Hmmm.

Nettle There, let's be friends. Why don't you take the rest of the cake away to have with your tea?

Compost Mmmm, 'ere, thanks. It is very nice. I'm sorry I was rude.

Nettle Don't worry, away you go!

Compost exits happily munching

Miss Nettle suddenly gets horrid again. She fingers her unusual brooch

Nettle (*to the audience*) HA! I'll teach that gardener he can't make a fool of me . . . (*to the doll*) won't I, eh, dolly?

She storms off, cackling away

The lights go down but a single light pauses momentarily on the doll. Its head turns to follow her off. For a cheap laugh it could put its tongue out too.

Black-out

SCENE 2

Lights come up to reveal Gloria standing centre stage holding a dish mop. She has a tea towel tucked into her apron string. She faces the audience and mimes washing up

Gloria (*calling off*) Egbert, what are you doing?

Egbert (*off*) A very important job, dear.

Gloria What?

Egbert (*off*) Just finishing off the last of the ice-cream.

Gloria We've had that ever since Sammy's party. You can't still be eating it?

Egbert comes on with ice-cream all over his mouth

Egbert I can. Yum. Funny his friends not eating anything.

Gloria Here.

She tosses him the tea towel; he wipes his mouth with it

Egbert Thanks.

Gloria No, I want you to dry up.

Egbert Oh.

Gloria The garden wants doing very badly too.

Egbert Really? I could do it really badly. I'm a rotten gardener.

Gloria I can't think where Compost could have got to. I don't think he's been in since the party.

Egbert No.

Gloria And Sammy's not himself. He's been in a daze for days.

Egbert A daysfadays?

Gloria He's usually so lively, but recently he's been half-asleep all day. Even you must have noticed.

Egbert Hmmm?

Gloria I said even you must have noticed.

Sadly Egbert seems to have got his hand stuck drying the bottom of a glass

Egbert Hmmm?

Gloria I said there's an elephant wearing your pyjamas doing a tap dance on the ceiling.

Egbert Quite.

Gloria Egbert, sometimes I ask myself if you can hear me . . . Egbert?

Egbert Sorry dear, I thought you were asking yourself.

Gloria What are we going to do about Sammy to get him back to normal?

Egbert Take him to the hospital?

Gloria No, maybe take him to the zoo, though.

Egbert I think they'd look after him better in hospital.

Gloria What did we do when we were young?

Egbert That's going back a bit!

Music 8: Flame Of Youth

Egbert	Do you remember all those faraway days?
Gloria	And how we filled them in a million ways?
Egbert	Climbing on the see-saw in the back of the park.
Gloria	Queuing up for fish and chips when it got dark.
Egbert	Your mother always used to put plaits in your hair.
Gloria	You tried to tie them to the back of a chair.
Egbert	When you first made your face up you looked more like a clown.
Gloria	You glued your legs to stop your socks falling down.
Both	But now that the flame of youth
	Is no more than an ember
	There's nothing more we like to do than
	Sit back and remember.
Egbert	Waiting in the classroom for school to begin
Gloria	Hiding the chalk before the teacher came in
Egbert	You took your teddy bear wherever you went
Gloria	And every exam you got a hundred percent.
	You ripped your trousers climbing a tree
	And had to walk backwards so your mum didn't see
Egbert	You always wanted a royal blue dress
	So we covered it in ink—
Both	Boy what a mess!
	Those were the happy days
	When we would never think
	We'd finish up together
	By the kitchen sink.

Gloria Do you think Sammy'll be all right?

Egbert (*staring upwards*) Yes, dear.

Gloria I do hope so. What are you looking for?

Egbert Just wondering if that tap-dancing elephant you spoke about had finished with my pyjamas.

Gloria Oh, Egbert, you are silly. Will you have a look at the garden then?

Egbert Now? It's a bit late. Anyway it's like a jungle at the moment, it gives me the creeps. How's this washing up coming along?

Gloria I think we've got the actions about right now.
Egbert Me too. Let's go and try it with real plates.

SCENE 3

*Lights come up slowly and we see the overgrown Magic Garden in UV light,
featuring amazing flowers, butterflies, spiders, caterpillars, snakes, etc. Also
discernible are a scarecrow and an old sundial; to one side is Compost's shed.
At first there is nice music—this fades away and more general lighting comes
up to suggest moonlight. Sammy is seated by the shed*

Sammy (*to the audience*) Hello, everyone, I'm keeping watch like Compost
   said. I don't know where he's been the last few weeks, but it hasn't been
   round here. I'm tired though, I haven't slept for ages.

Alice sneaks on

Alice (*calling softly*) Sam! Sammy, are you there?
Sammy (*to audience*) It's Alice! (*Calling*) Over here, by the shed.
Alice Hi! Anything happened yet?
Sammy You mean Miss Nettle? No, she still hasn't been.
Alice Do you think Compost was right?
Sammy I don't know, I wish he was here, I can't help thinking something's
   happened to him.
Alice Maybe he just took a sudden holiday?
Sammy Maybe . . . you're shaking, Alice. It's a bit spooky, isn't it?
Alice No, no, just a bit chilly, that's all.
Sammy I just boiled the kettle in the shed so we can have some tea if you
   like.

Alice steps into the shed

Alice Brill thinking. Is this the tea in the tin?
Sammy Yes, Compost's favourite.
Alice It looks like the bottom of a bird cage.
Sammy The milk's worse. It's been there for weeks.
Alice Do you want sugar?
Sammy There isn't any.
Alice There is, in this blue pot.

Alice emerges dipping her finger in a blue pot and then licking it

Sammy (*not looking round*) That's rat poison.
Alice Bleurghhh!
Sammy Shhh!
Alice Can't!
Sammy Alice, look!
Alice What is she up to?

   They watch as Miss Nettle creeps on

*She shiftily approaches the scarecrow and removes her odd brooch from its
jacket. She then looks to the sky towards the moon. She holds the brooch at an*

angle to direct the moonlight at the sundial. The sundial starts to glow and throb in a peculiar fashion. She makes a few mystic gestures then replaces the brooch on the scarecrow. The sundial returns to normal

Miss Nettle creeps off again

Alice Oh, wow.
Sammy Did we really see that?
Alice Oh, wow.
Sammy What happened?
Alice Oh, wow.
Sammy Alice, stop saying "oh, wow". What was it?
Alice Weird! Like some ritual ceremony.
Sammy That's the brooch she always wears! What was she doing with it?
Alice What was that message in your homework book?
Sammy The one about the sundial?
Sammy ⎫
Alice ⎬ (*realising together*) The sundial!
Sammy It sort of ties up!
Alice Oh, wow.
Sammy It just seems like a normal old stone lump to me. Well it does *now*, anyway. Maybe it was just a trick of the light.
Alice But why bother in the middle of the night?
Sammy Let's see that brooch.

They go over to the scarecrow. Sammy examines the brooch then hesitantly touches it. Reassured he removes it from the scarecrow

Alice Let's think about it at home.
Sammy No, nothing's going to happen now. Come on, we'll finish this tea first. Phew! It's not short of flavour!

Sammy sits at the base of the scarecrow. Cautiously Alice joins him

Alice I can't stay out too long.
Sammy (*thinking*) It doesn't make sense.

Suddenly a nasty animal shriek pierces the air. They both jump

Alice Sam!
Sammy Come on, Alice, that was only a bird or something.
Alice Does it have to make a noise like that?
Sammy Just think what Compost would say . . .

Music 5a: Remember There's Nothing To Be Scared Of (Reprise of Song 5)
   (*Singing*) A cat's got to call like a lion's got to roar
                 A snake's got to crawl like an eagle's got to soar
                 Night's got to fall at the end of every day
                 Don't let it all drive your common sense away.
                 Remember there's nothing to be scared of
                 Remember there's nothing there at all
                 Remember there's nothing to be scared of
                 Remember there's nothing there at all.

As the gentle tune reassures them both, suddenly the arm on the scarecrow swings down. Both jump up

Sammy ⎫ (*together*) AHH!
Alice ⎰

Sammy It's just the scarecrow.
Alice And you're telling me not to be frightened?
Sammy Huh. Funny, I don't remember this scarecrow before.
Alice Ugly old thing, isn't it?
Sammy Hmm.

Sammy is sitting down again but Alice is still looking at the scarecrow. It twitches, she jumps

Alice It moved!
Sammy What did?
Alice The scarecrow.
Sammy Alice, it's just a breeze.
Alice (*to the audience*) It moved, didn't it?
Sammy (*to the audience*) Don't let her try and scare you.
Alice It definitely moved.
Sammy Nonsense. (*To the audience*) If it moves, you'll tell us, right? I want to finish my tea.
Alice What time is it?
Sammy I haven't got my watch.
Alice Oh.
Sammy The sundial says it's about midnight.
Alice Oh.

The scarecrow twitches. Hopefully there is audience reaction. Sammy and Alice jump up

Sammy (*to the audience*) Where? I can't see it.
Alice (*to the audience*) Did it really move?
Sammy They're just saying it to scare us.
Alice (*to the audience*) Are you?

Audience should all shout "No". Sammy shouts "Oh yes you were". They shout "Oh no we weren't". This goes on for a while. Exasperated, Sammy and Alice sit down

Sammy It doesn't work. I don't believe them.
Alice Sam, how do sundials work?
Sammy Well the sun shines on the prong that sticks up and casts a shadow.
Alice But there isn't any sun at midnight. How could you tell the time?
Sammy Maybe it's a moondial.

The scarecrow moves again. Audience reaction

Sammy (*to audience*) Where?
Sammy ⎫ (*together*) Oh no it didn't ... (*For a few times*) Didn't, didn't,
Alice ⎰   didn't. (*Etc.*)

Alice (*to audience*) We're not scared by you.
Sammy (*to audience*) We're not going to believe you now.

The clock is heard chiming midnight

    Listen, it *is* midnight.
Alice Very loud, that clock of yours.
Sammy Alice, I told you, we haven't got a clock.
Alice So what's chiming then?
Sammy Funny, it seems to be coming from the sundial!

The scarecrow groans

Sammy The scarecrow!
Alice It's alive!
Sammy There's somebody in there!
Alice Sammy, leave it!

Sammy bravely goes up to the scarecrow, which keeps twitching. It has a face made of an old sack. Sammy darts in and snatches the sack off the top revealing a not-well-looking Compost, who speaks as if in pain

Compost Tea.
Sammy It's speaking!
Alice It's frightening!
Sammy }(*together*) It's Compost!
Alice
Compost Tea!
Alice He wants some of his tea.

Sammy holds a cup up to Compost's lips. Compost drinks

Sammy There.
Compost Tea.
Sammy (*to Alice*) Get the pot.

Alice goes to the shed to get the teapot

    (*To Compost*) Are you all right?
Compost Tea.

Alice returns, teapot in hand

Sammy Pour it in.

Alice tips the teapot spout into Compost's mouth

Alice (*to Sammy*) Can he talk?
Sammy (*to Compost*) Can you talk?
Compost Ubble, ubble, ubble.
Sammy What?
Alice (*listening intently*) get ... the ... tea ... pot ... out ... of ... my ... mouth!
Sammy Oh! Right! (*To Compost*) What are you doing here?
Compost Nettle's ... cake!

Sammy And we nearly ate it! Can you walk?
Compost Listen! . . . Sundial . . . use the brooch!

Sammy passes the brooch up to Compost

Sammy This?
Compost Ahhh! Keep it back! Use it on the sundial!
Alice You mean we have to hold it up?
Compost Yes, YES!

Sammy holds the brooch up. At first nothing happens

Sammy It's not working.
Alice Move it over a bit.
Compost Ahhh! There!
Sammy What's happening?

Once again the lightbeams form and the sundial throbs. Compost is gradually released. Weird sounds build up

Alice (*to Compost*) Are you feeling any better?
Compost Don't know.
Alice Keep holding it, Sam!
Compost That's it, it's like a big hand is letting go of me!
Sammy Is that enough?
Compost Keep going, it's working, I'm getting freer.
Alice Steady!
Compost Nearly . . . and there! I feel light as a bird! I could do a marathon!

Compost steps down, but then stumbles. Sammy and Alice catch him

Sammy Legs a bit wobbly, eh?
Alice Sammy, look!

The sundial continues to glow and the noise still builds. The Flower-children at the background start coming alive. What starts off with a few movements can build into a whole dance number. They can either be really slick and get tap-dancing as they find their feet, or they can be all wobbly as they try to walk for the first time in years. They gradually turn from flowers into children wearing old-fashioned clothes

Compost (*to Flower-children*) Look at you all! (*To Sammy and Alice*) Help me get them cleaned up.

The music continues through this section as Compost introduces the rather shy, bewildered Flower-children to Sammy and Alice. There's a little chorus that keeps cropping up too

Hello! Don't be shy! Remember me, old Compost? This is Polly, the oldest, and this is her brother Merrick here.
Flower-kid Chorus Oooo . . . it's nice to see you again
Oooo . . . I've missed you all
Oooo . . . We're all together again
Oooo . . . I've missed you all.

As more children come alive they join in this chorus. Compost continues

Compost And here's Toby who's a nuisance, never would eat his fertiliser! And Isabel who used to sing for me after school, hello Isabel!

Repeat chorus

This looks like Jess to me, remember me, Jess? Compost? I remember you and all your mischief. And who's this little last person, eh? It's Lucinda, my own sweetheart.

Repeat chorus

Well don't be shy, everybody! You're all right now. Somebody say something.

Lucinda Where's my doll?

There's a nice little magic noise and the rag doll flies over to Lucinda. (It can slide down a thread or something.) The sundial dies away again. The brooch is left lying on it

Compost Now, just take it steady all of you. There's no more standing out in all weathers for you lot; we'll find somewhere for you all to live . . .

Miss Nettle suddenly appears and the nice music stops

The children all cower behind Sammy and Compost

Nettle Ah! You meddling fools. Do you know what you've done?
Compost One more word and I know what *I'm* going to do.
Nettle Silence, you horticultural horror.
Alice Sammy, the brooch!!

Sadly Miss Nettle gets there first

Nettle You really shouldn't be playing with things like this, should you? You have no idea of the power it unlocks!

Everybody shows great concern at this, emitting the odd distressed "Argh" and "Ooh" and even the occasional "Eeek"

What a pathetic gathering you are! I shan't forget or forgive this.
Sammy There's something you should know, Miss Nettle.
Nettle Little Mr Sammy Smartipants, eh? What should I know?
Sammy I don't think anybody here likes you.

What looks like a throwaway comment has a momentary effect on Miss Nettle before she shrugs it off . . . This effect is not lost on Sammy

Let's find out. Does anybody like her?
Nettle So what?
Sammy Well, don't moan when you never get any birthday cards, that's all.
Nettle For that I'm going to turn you into a mushroom.
Compost She never had a birthday card in her life.
Alice Hey, maybe if she had, she wouldn't be so horrid.

Miss Nettle is not enjoying these revelations. However, she reassures her self-confidence again with a spot of malice

Nettle Well I haven't, so I am, so there. And now you will become my botanical babes again!

She holds the brooch up and the sundial glows as before. However, she can't seem to exercise control and suddenly drops the brooch as it glows red hot. Miss Nettle recoils in shock. Slowly and horribly she turns into a nettle. The sundial returns to normal

Sammy Look! It's gone wrong!
Alice It's horrible.
Sammy Instead of changing us, *she's* changed!
Alice She's changed into a real nettle!

Everybody cheers as one would expect

Compost 'ere, what are we going to do with all you lot then?
Sammy Take them upstairs, raid the larder and clean them up.
Compost Your Mum'll go potty with this lot.
Sammy Potty's one thing, this is more important. Go on.

Compost and the Flower-children go off

Alice, if only we had somebody to look after them all!
Alice Like who? Even Miss Nettle's gone.
Sammy Hmmm. I wonder how long it lasts?
Alice Those other kids were trapped for years. It's vile.
Sammy We can't just leave her like this, you know. We have to try and turn her back.
Alice But we don't know how!
Sammy We've got the brooch, haven't we?
Alice Even if you managed, how do we know she wouldn't be the same?
Sammy Look, you know Compost said she'd never had any birthday cards ever?
Alice So?
Sammy It was her birthday the same day as mine, suppose we had a late card for her? It might make her feel wanted for once and she'd be nicer.
Alice A card signed by loads of people?
Sammy Yeah, that'd be brilliant. Only where do we get one?
Alice Actually we've got one. It was for you, but I hadn't put your name on it yet.

Alice produces the card signed by the audience (in the interval, remember?)

Sammy That's it. Fill in her name so it says "Happy Birthday, Miss Nettle".
Alice Do you want to sign it too?
Sammy Yeah.

The card is prepared

Right then, now for the tricky bit!

Alice How do we know you won't become a nettle too?
Sammy It's a risk I'll just have to take! (*To the audience*) Shall I risk it?

Audience reaction

Here goes then.

Sammy holds up the brooch again. At first nothing happens, but then suddenly the sundial glows. It makes a very ominous new set of noises. Sammy and Alice see the sundial fade down, and then see Miss Nettle start to resume normality

Sammy Let's leave the card and hide, I don't want to be about when she's changed.
Alice Neat thinking, Sammy.
Sammy That's me.

They scarper off as Miss Nettle starts tottering about

Nettle What ... what's happened ...? Oh yes that sundial, the horrible children, all shouting they hate me, wait till I get my hands on them ... what's this? Happy Birthday Miss Nettle? I bet no one's signed it, because nobody likes me. (*She opens the card and starts reading out some names*) Oh! I see [name 1] has signed. Well what a nice person, [s/he] would. And so has [name 2]. If I met them I could well be tempted to give them a sweetie or two. (*She has some real unspooky non-poisonous sweets on her. To the audience*) Do you know who [name 1] is? And [name 2]? How about [name 3]? Who else signed? Did you? (*etc., etc. giving out sweets*) ... and who's this one? Sammy Matthews? *Not* Sammy Smartipants Matthews! And Alice? Revolting children. Aren't they? No? Are you sure?

Sammy and Alice enter

Sammy Er, hello! Come on, Alice.
Nettle (*to Sammy*) You! What are you doing here now?
Sammy I saw you giving out sweets to people who signed your card.
Nettle So?
Alice We signed it too.
Nettle Hmmmph. (*To the audience*) Do you think I should give them a sweet? There you are then.
Sammy Thanks.
Alice Thank you.
Sammy So what are you going to do now then, Miss Nettle?
Nettle What do you mean?
Sammy Well let's face it, you can't turn umpteen kids into flowers and get away with it.
Alice And there's the poisoned cake at the party.
Sammy Why did you do it?
Nettle Because, because, you were all so happy being children, and having parties and fun, and I ... I never had anything like that.
Alice Well you've sure blown it now!
Sammy Intimidation, attempted homicide, protection, it's an open-and-

shut case, doll. I'll be presenting my report to the D.A. first thing in the morning. You have the right to an attorney.

Nettle What on earth?

Alice What Sammy means is that you won't be allowed to stay here.

Nettle But where else could I go? I've always been here since I was a little girl.

Sammy Haven't you any family at all?

Nettle No.

Warning, this is all starting to get a bit tear-jerky now!

I was left here on the door step in a little crib made out of a *Swan and Edgar* shoe box when I was a tiny little girl. I've never had anyone.

Alice Supposing we could find you a family of your own?

Nettle Of my very own?

Sammy, Alice and Miss Nettle are all starting to be sniffily weepy

Sammy But you'd have to look after them.

Nettle Yes, oh yes.

Sammy And supposing you could stay here?

Nettle Yes, oh yes, oh yes.

Sammy Is it worth another sweet?

Nettle Here, take them all.

Sammy I couldn't. I'll leave you one.

Nettle One?

Sammy Here's what you've got to do.

Nettle What?

Sammy Go and offer your last sweet to Compost.

Nettle To Compost?

Sammy Away you go, and *good luck!*

A bewildered Miss Nettle sets off

Alice What was all that about?

Sammy Alice, do you know nothing of elementary para-psychology?

Alice I hope it all turns out all right. Hey, you've still got that brooch!

Sammy Oh! We'd better smash it to be sure.

They start trying to break it when Egbert comes out

Egbert What's that noise?

Alice Sorry if we disturbed you.

Egbert Never mind. I was stuck on the problem for the catalytic ray disbander for my molecular regrouping synthesiser. What's that?

Sammy Oh nothing, we've got to break it, that's all.

Egbert Let me see . . . good grief! Four point seven nine diffraction at two seven eight S.A.R. . . . that's standard Amstrong resonance of course . . .

Sammy⎱
Alice ⎰ (*together*) Of course!

Egbert This could be it! May I have it? If you don't want it! I'll need to defraturise it I'm afraid!

Alice You mean break it?

Egbert That too.

Sammy You take it, Dad!

Egbert Yippee deedle dee!

Egbert goes off very happily

Sammy At least there shouldn't be any more ghosts and things to scare you now.

Alice I wasn't scared at all. *You* were.

Sammy I wasn't. (*To the audience*) I bet you lot were!

Alice What do you do to stop yourself being scared then?

Sammy It's a little song I sing, listen:

Music 10: I'm Not Scared

(*Singing*)   I'm not scared, I'm not scared
Nothing frightens me
If things go bump in the night
One thing I don't feel is fright.
I'm not scared, I'm not scared
I'm as brave as can be
I couldn't be afraid if I was paid 'cause
Nothing frightens me.

Sammy talks as the music continues

(*Speaking*) What do you do then, Alice?

Alice Funnily enough I sing this . . .

(*Singing*)   I'm not scared, I'm not scared
Nothing frightens me
If things go bump in the night
One thing I don't feel is fright.
I'm not scared, I'm not scared
I'm as brave as can be
I couldn't be afraid if I was paid 'cause
Nothing frightens me.

Sammy Do you find though, that it's even better if a whole lot of people sing it?

Alice Every time, but where are we going to find a lot of people?

Sammy and Alice realise:

(*To the audience*) Of course! You lot!

Sammy Will you sing it with us? To make it easy we've even got the words here!

The words are displayed in whatever way is most convenient. Sammy and Alice do song with audience. Then split up audience, Sammy's half sing while Alice's half have to pull scarey faces at them, then vice versa, call it a draw, etc.

There *is* one thing that frightens me a little bit.
Alice What?
Sammy How am I going to explain to my Mum that I'm having all these new friends to stay?

Sammy and Alice exit

Compost enters

Compost (*to audience*) Hello, my little forget-me-nots! What a day it's been, eh? I had hoped to sow some carrots, but do you know why I couldn't?

Audience should by now readily reply about needles and threads

No, because I was a scarecrow—you haven't been paying attention, have you? It's nice to have all my little friends back with me, but to be honest, I don't know how I'm going to look after them all. Suppose they get the measles? Mind you, if they got green fly I could handle it.

In comes a very humble Miss Nettle

Nettle Hello, Compost.
Compost Oh hello, I see you haven't been weeded out yet?
Nettle Would you like a sweet?
Compost Oh yes please. Oh, it's your last one.
Nettle I'd like you to have it.
Compost Well, that is kind! Lovely. (*He pops sweet into his mouth*)
Nettle Remember that poisoned cake I gave you?

Compost coughs his sweet out

I just wanted to say I'm sorry.
Compost (*suspicious*) What is all this?
Nettle Please believe me!
Compost 'ere, I thought you were a nettle.
Nettle No, Sammy turned me back. He said I had to come and see you about a family to look after.
Compost A family? You mean my little friends? Here now, wait a minute. You've always been horrid to kiddies, and besides I'm looking after them, so there.
Nettle Oh. Oh, I see. I'll just say goodbye, then.
Compost Goodbye? Where are you going?
Nettle I don't know, but if I can't look after the children I can't stay here. I'll just go and pack my one or two pathetic belongings into a small cardboard suitcase and quietly leave through the back door turning round to take one farewell glance at the house that's been my only home since I was a tiny child.
Compost (*wiping his eyes*) This is worse than weeding the onion patch!
Nettle I understand if nobody wants me here and won't permit me to try and make amends for all the unforgivable things I've done. I've only my own self to blame if no one likes me, so I'll just go now.
Compost I never said I didn't like you.

Nettle You said I was a mean, horrid, selfish, nasty, unpleasant, antisocial, bad-tempered, domineering, repugnant, greedy, uncooperative, twisted, evil old bat.

Compost I still didn't say I didn't like you.

Nettle Do you mean?

Compost Only if ...

Nettle And if ...

Compost We've talked enough, bring your face here.

Nettle Why?

Compost I want to kiss it.

Just as they have a kiss:

the entire rest of the cast come on

Rest of Company Hey, Compost! ... Urghh! He's kissing Miss Nettle!

Compost No, no, no, I was just borrowing some of her lipstick.

Sammy You'll never guess what?

Alice It's brilliant!

Sammy Dad's invented a thingy-whatsit.

Egbert An activated enzyme catalyst molecular distortion regrouping synthesiser.

Compost I had one of those but the wheels fell off.

Sammy And they've paid him a massive cheque.

Gloria So we're thinking of converting the big tumble-down garage into a home for all these children.

Sammy Providing we can get some foster-parents for them.

Compost Er, um, well, I'd marry Miss Nettle as long as she promises not to give me any more poisoned cake.

Nettle And I'll marry Compost providing he promises not to tell those jokes again.

Sammy Looks like we're on course for a happy ending.

Compost (*to Miss Nettle*) Promise?

Everybody else breathes in expectantly

Nettle I promise.

Everybody else sighs, relieved

(*to Compost*) Do you promise?

Everybody else breathes in again

Compost ... No.

All but Compost Huh?!

Compost Only kidding!

Finale Medley: Remember There's Nothing To Be Scared Of
and/or I'm Not Scared

Company   If you hear a creaking in the night
                     It's only a skeleton touching his toes

If a cold breeze then gives you a fright
It's only a werewolf blowing his nose
If you hear a tapping on the window
If you hear a rapping on the door
It could be a spook or a vampire bat
But it won't be anything worse than that
Remember there's nothing to be scared of
Remember there's nothing there at all
Remember there's nothing to be scared of
Remember there's nothing there at all.

I'm Not Scared

Sammy I'm not scared I'm not scared
Nothing frightens me
If things go bump in the night
One thing I don't feel is fright
I'm not scared I'm not scared
I'm as brave as can be
I couldn't be afraid if I was paid 'cause
Nothing frightens me.

A spot of bowing and everyone toddles off to rapturous applause and cries of "Author, Author" etc. etc.

CURTAIN

FURNITURE AND PROPERTY LIST

ACT I

SCENE 1

On stage: Doormat outside Sammy's house

Off stage: Book **(Egbert)**
Broom **(Miss Nettle)**

Personal: **Sammy and his schoolfriends:** satchels/schoolbooks

SCENE 2

On stage: Nil

SCENE 3

On stage: Sofa
Television
Telly aerial
Table. *On it:* lamp, Sammy's schoolbooks
Sideboard (optional)

Off stage: Schoolbooks **(Alice)**
Rag doll (with tinkling bell) **(Stage Management)**

Personal: **Egbert:** book
Gloria: slippers

SCENE 4

On stage: Nil

Off stage: Schoolbooks **(Sammy's friends)**
Large pile of paper **(Bridget)**

Personal: **Sammy:** satchel, notebook
Alice: schoolbooks

SCENE 5

On stage: Table. *On it:* cloth, numerous bowls, scales, ladles, cookery book
Overhead cupboard, with bag of flour or similar substance in it

Personal: **Miss Nettle:** brooch

SCENE 6

On stage: Sammy's bed. *On it:* sheet
Diary
Satchel. *In it:* notebook

SCENE 7

On stage: Unnaturally large flowers

INTERVAL

Off stage: Large birthday card and pen **(brought round by Alice)**

ACT II

SCENE 1

On stage: Sofa
Television
Telly aerial
Table. *On it:* lamp
Sideboard (optional)

Off stage: Rag doll **(Stage Management)**
Huge cake **(Miss Nettle)**
Bottle of pop **(Egbert)**
Plates **(Miss Nettle)**

Personal: **Miss Nettle:** brooch

SCENE 2

Personal: **Gloria:** apron, dish mop, tea towel

SCENE 3

On stage: Large flowers **(Flower-children)**
Scarecrow **(Compost)**
Sundial
Shed

Off stage: Blue pot **(Alice)**
Tea cups **(Alice)**
Teapot **(Alice)**
Rag doll **(Stage Management)**
Large birthday card **(Alice)**

Personal: **Scarecrow/Compost:** brooch
Miss Nettle: sweets

LIGHTING PLOT

Practical fittings required: UV lighting (optional)
Various simple interior and exterior settings

ACT I, Scene 1

To open: Black-out

| Cue 1 | After Magic Garden Theme ends | (Page 1) |
| | *Sunny exterior lighting comes up* | |

| Cue 2 | **Miss Nettle** cackles off | (Page 5) |
| | *Fade lights* | |

ACT I, Scene 2

To open: General exterior lighting

| Cue 3 | **Sammy:** "... homework to do. Yuck!" | (Page 8) |
| | *Fade lights* | |

ACT I, Scene 3

To open: General interior lighting

| Cue 4 | **Sammy** and **Alice** chew their biros thoughtfully | (Page 10) |
| | *Black-out* | |

| Cue 5 | **Sammy:** "Oh no, it's the lights again!" | (Page 10) |
| | *Lights flicker back on* | |

| Cue 6 | **Alice:** "Oh real wow ... ah!" | (Page 11) |
| | *Lights flicker again* | |

| Cue 7 | **Compost:** "... table! Hur, hur, hur, hur, hur" | (Page 15) |
| | *Fade lights* | |

ACT I, Scene 4

To open: General exterior lighting

| Cue 8 | **Alice:** "Sam? *Come on!*" | (Page 17) |
| | *Fade lights* | |

ACT I, Scene 5

| Cue 9 | After Magic Garden Theme ends | (Page 17) |
| | *General interior lighting* | |

| Cue 10 | **Miss Nettle** storms off ... | (Page 19) |
| | *Lights go down* | |

ACT I, SCENE 6

To open: General interior lighting

| *Cue* 11 | **Gloria** goes | (Page 20) |

Lights go down

| *Cue* 12 | **Sammy** holds the sheet above his head ... | (Page 20) |

Spot on **Sammy**

| *Cue* 13 | **Sammy:** "... go 'Ow' when you biff them." | (Page 20) |

Lighting increases gradually till end of scene

| *Cue* 14 | **Compost:** "This way then." | (Page 21) |

Fade lights

ACT I, SCENE 7

To open: Soft backlighting

| *Cue* 15 | **Sammy:** "... I'm going to save you!" | (Page 23) |

Lights go down

ACT II, SCENE 1

To open: Darkness

| *Cue* 16 | **Sammy** puts a table lamp on | (Page 24) |

Low interior lighting

| *Cue* 17 | **School kids** leap out of nowhere | (Page 24) |

General interior lighting

| *Cue* 18 | **Sammy:** "It's all right, it's just that ..." | (Page 26) |

Black-out

| *Cue* 19 | **Kevin:** "Whooo!" | (Page 26) |

Lights come up

| *Cue* 20 | **Miss Nettle** storms off cackling away | (Page 31) |

Lights go down, but single spot remains on rag doll, then black-out

ACT II, SCENE 2

To open: General interior lighting

| *Cue* 21 | **Egbert** and **Gloria** go off | (Page 33) |

Fade lights

ACT II, SCENE 3

To open: UV lighting

| *Cue* 22 | As nice music fades away | (Page 33) |

Moonlight

| *Cue* 23 | **Miss Nettle** holds the brooch ... at the moonlight | (Page 34) |

Sundial starts to glow

| *Cue* 24 | **Miss Nettle** ... replaces the brooch on the scarecrow | (Page 34) |

Sundial returns to normal

Cue 25	**Sammy:** "What's happening?"	(Page 37)
	Lightbeams form on the sundial	
Cue 26	**Alice:** "Sammy, look!"	(Page 37)
	Sundial continues to glow	
Cue 27	Rag doll flies over to Lucinda	(Page 38)
	Sundial dies away again	
Cue 28	**[Miss Nettle]** holds the brooch up	(Page 39)
	Sundial glows; brooch glows red hot	
Cue 29	**[Miss Nettle]** turns into a nettle	(Page 39)
	Sundial returns to normal	
Cue 30	**Sammy** holds up the brooch again ...	(Page 40)
	Sundial glows, then fades down	

EFFECTS PLOT

ACT I

Cue 1   After Magic Garden Theme   (Page 1)
           School handbell rings

Cue 2   **Sammy** and **Alice** chew their biros thoughtfully   (Page 10)
           An eerie wind whispers

Cue 3   **[Sammy** and **Alice]** try and settle down ...   (Page 11)
           Creepy wind noise grows
           Nasty green hand appears behind the sofa

Cue 4   **Sammy** screams sharply   (Page 11)
           Hand goes away

Cue 5   **Sammy:** "... this homework done now."   (Page 12)
           A clock chimes nine

Cue 6   **Miss Nettle** cackles off stage ...   (Page 13)
           Enormous echoing footsteps

Cue 7   **All but Sammy:** "Eh?"   (Page 16)
           School bell goes

Cue 8   **Miss Nettle** is fingering her odd brooch   (Page 18)
           Spooky wind starts up

Cue 9   **Miss Nettle** storms out   (Page 19)
           Magic wind noises build up
           Objects fly about (optional)

Cue 10   **Sammy:** "I wonder what time it is?"   (Page 20)
           The clock chimes midnight

Cue 11   **Sammy:** "'magic sundial'?"   (Page 20)
           Distant thunder rumbles, eerie wind noise starts

ACT II

Cue 12   **Sammy:** "It doesn't make sense."   (Page 34)
           A nasty animal shriek pierces the air

Cue 13   **Sammy:** "We're not going to believe you now."   (Page 36)
           The clock is heard chiming midnight

Cue 14   **Sammy:** "What's happening?"   (Page 37)
           Weird sounds build up

Cue 15   **Alice:** "Sammy, look!"   (Page 37)
           Noise builds

Cue 16   **Lucinda:** "Where's my doll?"   (Page 38)
          There is a nice little magic noise
          Doll flies down

Cue 17   ... suddenly the sundial glows   (Page 40)
          Ominous new set of noises

MADE AND PRINTED IN GREAT BRITAIN BY
LATIMER TREND & COMPANY LTD PLYMOUTH

MADE IN ENGLAND